IMAGES
of America

NORCROSS

This photograph of College Avenue in Norcross was taken some time after 1914. It shows, from left to right, the Norcross Methodist Church, Norcross Elementary School, and Norcross High School. At the writing of this book, the church building was still standing, but the schools were demolished in the latter part of the 20th century, and Lillian Webb Park had been developed in the area. These buildings, along with the railroad depot and Thrasher Park, were major landmarks in the town, with the high school known as the "Castle on the Hill." (Courtesy of Billy and Joann Weathers.)

ON THE COVER: Members of the Norcross Methodist Church gather for a camp meeting along the banks of the Chattahoochee River at Jones Bridge around 1919. Tom Rochester (back row, second from right, with cap) was the cook for this gathering. The tradition of camp meetings for this church extend back to the days when it was known as Flint Hill, and camp meetings were held regularly between 1825 and 1862. (Courtesy of Michelle Morgan.)

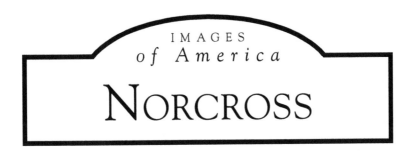

IMAGES
of America

NORCROSS

Edith Holbrook Riehm, Gene Ramsay,
and Cate Kitchen

ARCADIA
PUBLISHING

Published by Arcadia Publishing
Charleston, South Carolina

Library of Congress Control Number: 2011920416

For all general information, please contact Arcadia Publishing:
Telephone 843-853-2070
Fax 843-853-0044
E-mail sales@arcadiapublishing.com
For customer service and orders:
Toll-Free 1-888-313-2665

Visit us on the Internet at www.arcadiapublishing.com

To Irene Crapo, Martha and John Adams, Noye Nesbit,
Allen P. Francis, Harold Medlock, and Elliott Brack,
who laid the groundwork so others could follow

CONTENTS

ACKNOWLEDGMENTS

Thanks to all in Norcross and around the United States who helped in assembling these photographs and the related text, including Al Karnitz; Amelia and Michael Welch; Ann Newton Barker; Annette Kelly Kellett; Arlene Beckles; the James G. Kenan Research Center at the Atlanta History Center; Barbara Eger; Betty Scott Jarrett; Bill Barks; Billy and Joann Weathers; Bob Basford; Bob Pritchard; Bonnie Fitzpatrick; Bucky Johnson; Buddy Ray; Carl Mauldin; Carl and Sherry Johnson; Carolyn Collins; Carol MacGregor; Charles Carroll; Charlie Riehm; Christ Church Episcopal; Chuck Cimarik; Cindy Flynn; City of Norcross; Connie Weathers; Danny Lay; David McLeroy; David Sumner; Deborah Walker Little; Dr. James Woods; Dwayne Higgins; Ed Moulder; Edwin Johnson; Elliott Brack; Evelyn Nesbit Norman; Frances Mitchell; Fred Lindquist; Geoff Hammett; Special Collections and Archives, Georgia State University; the Georgia Tech Foundation's *Images and Memories Photograph Collection* (1985); Gwinnett Fire Station No. 1; Gwinnett Historical Society; Hopewell Missionary Baptist Church; Horace Simpson; Jack and Delicia Reynolds; Jane Holbrook; Jeff Kitchen; Jennifer Gregg; Jerry Cloer; Jimmy and Joye Nesbit; Joan and Carl Garner Jr.; Jimmy and Linda Garner; John Adams; John Day; John Landstrom; Johnny Lawler; Joyce Davenport Clark; Julie Eskeridge; Julie Rutkowski; Kathy Kitz; Ken Weatherford; Kim Civins; Krista Lay; Leigh Mehas; Lillian Hicks Webb; Liz and Dodger DeLeon; Lori Medlock Anderson; Louis Bentley; Louise Ivy Clark; Lynn Hamilton Griffeth; Marilyn Meacham; Marilyn Somers; Meryl Wilkerson; Michelle Morgan; Misty Wilson; Mount Carmel Methodist Church; Nate Brown; Norcross First Baptist Church; Norcross First United Methodist Church; Norcross High School; Norcross Lions Club; Norcross Lodge No. 228 of the Free and Accepted Masons; Norcross Police Department; Norcross Presbyterian Church; Norcross Old Timers Baseball Association; Norcross Garden Club; Ovella Jackson; Pam Hopper; Pat Eidt; Penelope Nesbit Reed; Ranae Heaven; Ray Cobb; Reuben Gant Jr.; Richard Garner; Richard Sudderth; Rip Robertson; Robert Byars; Rufus Dunnigan; Sally Toole; Sandie Nesbit Speer; Sara and Pierre Levy; Shannon Byers; Shelby and Ron Horn; Shirley Letson; Skip Nau; South Caroliniana Library at the University of South Carolina in Columbia; Susan and Jerry Brown; Teresa Hinton Cantrell; Terry Hoye; Thomas Ivy; Tina Marie DeVincenzo; Tixie Fowler; Tonya Epps; Venusnep Photography; Virginia Nesbit; and William M. Smith.

INTRODUCTION

Long before the first white settlers came to the area, the Creek and Cherokee Native American nations inhabited the lands that became Norcross and Gwinnett County. The county was created by the State of Georgia in 1818, carved out of land southeast of the Chattahoochee River that had been ceded by the Native Americans after the War of 1812. During that war, the first road in the area, the original Peachtree Road, was built to connect two frontier forts, and it came through the middle of what would become the town of Norcross some years later.

Lotteries were held in the 1820s to allocate the newly available land to pioneer families. Their roots, and those of their enslaved labor force, extend into the 21st century. The first settlement by the Europeans in the area was called Pinckneyville, named for a South Carolina political figure, Charles Pinckney, who visited the area around the time the county was established. An inn at a stop along the stage coach route from Augusta, Georgia, into Alabama was established on present day Medlock Bridge Road by the 1830s and served as the center of this community, along with Mount Carmel Methodist Church, which was organized in 1828.

By the mid-19th century, the nearest major population center (as today) was Atlanta, which was a railroad hub for the southeastern United States by 1860. There were plans to build a railroad from Atlanta to Richmond, Virginia, in the late 1850s, but the construction of the railroad was delayed due to the rising tensions that led to the Civil War. After the war, that railroad, the Richmond & Danville, was laid from Atlanta to Charlotte, North Carolina, and beyond.

As railroad construction got underway, pioneer Atlanta settler John J. Thrasher bought Gwinnett County land lot no. 254, consisting of about 250 acres in the area of the first planned stop on the railroad north of Atlanta. He laid out a new city on his land, auctioned off lots, and obtained a charter for the town from the State of Georgia in October 1870, making it the second city founded in Gwinnett County. Thrasher named the town after his longtime Atlanta friend Jonathan Norcross, who had served as mayor of Atlanta in the 1850s and was viewed as a primary founder of that city (as was Thrasher). The town of Norcross was located where the Peachtree Road crossed the new railroad, near the site of the Hopewell Missionary Baptist Church, which had been founded by former slaves in 1865.

Thrasher marketed Norcross as "Atlanta's Favorite Summer Resort," and he built the Brunswick Hotel as a destination for visitors who came via the railroad. It became a favored spot for Atlantans escaping the heat and bustle of the city, enjoying the hotel's porches with its rocking chairs and its renowned chicken potpie. With the railroad and the new town came new opportunities, and families from nearby communities such as Pinckneyville and Flint Hill soon moved to Norcross, becoming store owners, entrepreneurs, and railroaders. Several churches with origins in the farming communities that predated Norcross also moved to the town, at first using the Community House for their meetings and, later in the 19th century, building their own houses of worship.

In 1878, Thrasher moved on to his next opportunity in South Carolina, but the town he founded thrived, becoming the trading center for the area, and its families produced professional baseball players, soldiers, preachers, teachers, entrepreneurs, and civic leaders. Local farmers shipped their cotton out of the railroad depot in downtown Norcross, and furniture and harness businesses shipped their products throughout the southeastern United States. Two additional hotels were built, as well as retail stores, a post office, and blacksmith shops.

The 20th century brought a new form of transportation, the automobile, and the first such device assembled in the southeastern United States, the short-lived Nor-X, was made in a Norcross factory funded by Edward Buchanan, a local boy who became a baron of Wall Street. (Unfortunately, his fall from riches was even more dramatic than his ascent.) Norcross was bypassed as major highways were built in the region in the mid-20th century, and prosperity waned in the area, hard hit by the droughts and boll weevil infestation of the 1920s and the onset of the Great Depression in the 1930s. With the decline in train travel, Norcross lost its appeal as a destination and became a sleepy Southern town, retaining its small-town charm as well as most of its historic commercial buildings and Victorian-era homes.

In the 1960s and 1970s, the creation of the Technology Park/Atlanta business park and the construction of Peachtree Industrial Boulevard, on the edge of Norcross, helped to spur the explosive growth that characterized the last quarter of the 20th century in Gwinnett County. Fortunately, most of this development also skirted around Norcross's historic district. To further protect the downtown, the central part of Norcross was placed in the National Registry of Historic Places in 1980. Today, Norcross, with its revitalized downtown and numerous well-preserved buildings from bygone days, is once again a destination for many in the metro Atlanta area, a jewel in the crown of Gwinnett County.

This book is a visual history telling the story of Norcross, Georgia, through the lenses of many cameras spanning its 140 years and more. But it is not just a photograph book—it is also is a documented oral history comprised of the recollections of many in the Norcross community who shared with the authors their family photographs, histories, and memories. It tells the stories of those who skirted the law and those whose job was to uphold it, of sports stars who had long and storied careers as well as those who burned out after a brief time in the spotlight. It tells of men and women, blacks and whites, young and old, who gave of their lives to build their community, their houses of worship, and their families. This book is an effort by old-timers and newcomers, all sharing a home in the wonderful city of Norcross.

One

PIONEER SETTLERS

The man with the white beard in the center of this photograph is Norman F. Cooledge (1823–1897). He was born in Vermont and moved as a young man to Cotton Hill, Georgia, where he took a job as a schoolmaster. In the early 1870s, he moved to Norcross, and he ran a school here (shown) for 20 years. (Courtesy of the James G. Kenan Research Center at the Atlanta History Center.)

During the War of 1812, the Georgia Militia commissioned a few local men to build a road between two forts to allow transfer of military supplies. William Nesbit (1789–1863), one of the builders of this original Peachtree Road, is pictured. He served Gwinnett County after its creation in 1818 as sheriff and state legislator. (Courtesy of the Nesbit family.)

An inn (shown) was established in southwestern Gwinnett County around the time the county was founded in 1818 to serve stagecoach passengers and other wayfarers. The building no longer exists; it was on the western side of Medlock Bridge Road, near the current location of Norcross Presbyterian Church. (Courtesy of Annette Kelly Kellett.)

Georgia counties are subdivided into numbered militia districts. District 406, in southwestern Gwinnett County where Norcross is located, was named Pinckneyville after Charles Pinckney, a noted South Carolina politician who traveled through the area around the time the county was founded. (Courtesy of the South Caroliniana Library, University of South Carolina, Columbia, SC.)

CHARLES PINCKNEY
Nat 1758 - Ob 1824

Gainum Rakestraw and his wife, Sarah Sammon Rakestraw (shown), were early settlers in the Pinckneyville area, owning land located on either side of the current North Peachtree Street in Norcross north of Sunset Drive. The Rakestraws were charter members of the Norcross Baptist Church, which was organized in 1872. (Courtesy of Norcross First Baptist Church.)

Stephen Tilly (S.T.) McElroy (1844–1929), pioneer Norcross-area settler, is pictured with his mother, Margaret Tilly McElroy, and three descendants, covering five generations. They are pictured at the family homestead, Flint Hill, on South Peachtree Road in Norcross. McElroy's father, William, purchased this house and approximately 500 acres in July 1864 from Hendley Harris. Margaret McElroy had inherited slaves from father Stephen Tilly's estate. Tilly was a DeKalb County pioneer settler who owned a large plantation and a mill. William McElroy did not agree with slavery, but rather than free these slaves, he sold them, using the proceeds to buy Flint Hill and the surrounding acreage. William McElroy died a few months after this purchase. In 1870, his son, S.T. McElroy, moved his wife, Laura Lively McElroy, and family to Flint Hill from DeKalb County. In 1914, S.T. McElroy wrote a brief but informative autobiography, including details about his journey home from service in the Civil War, difficulties encountered after the war, and his long life in Norcross. (Courtesy of Evelyn Nesbit Norman.)

Pictured at Flint Hill is a reunion of S.T. McElroy's family. McElroy overcame losing part of his left leg in the Battle of Baker's Creek, near Vicksburg, Mississippi, during the Civil War to succeed in family life (he was married four times, outliving his first three wives, and had eight children) and in business (establishing a sawmill, furniture manufacturing firm, and other businesses). (Courtesy of Evelyn Nesbit Norman.)

Sylvester Nesbit (1824–1902) was the son of pioneer Gwinnett road builder and sheriff William Nesbit. William and his wife, Caroline "Carrie" Lively Nesbit (1843–1939), daughter of pioneer Norcross settler Milton C. Lively, are shown. They had a farm on the west bank of the Chattahoochee River downstream from the McAfee/Holcomb bridge where they ran the Nesbit Ferry. (Courtesy of Evelyn Nesbit Norman.)

orge L. Bell, who was judge of , and is the mother of Judge Atlanta. She is 82 years old.

Thomas Hardaway Jones (1779–1877) arrived in Gwinnett County in 1827. Pictured are his son Hilliard "Clarke" Jones, his daughter-in-law Mrs. George L. Jones (Anna), and his daughter Mary Helena Jones. In the summer of 1864, young Clarke was killed at the family home by Federal troops who were pursuing his brother George, a captain in the Confederate cavalry who had stopped by the homestead. (Courtesy of Sara and Pierre Levy.)

Hampshire Jones (1827–1908), whose grave marker in Hopewell Missionary Baptist Church Cemetery is shown, was a slave owned by Thomas Hardaway Jones. After Thomas's son Clarke Jones was killed by Federal troops, Hampshire walked a 10-mile round trip. Under the cover of darkness, he went to the home of Thomas's son on the Chattahoochee River and fetched Jones's daughter-in-law to help the grieving family. (Courtesy of the Authors.)

Hopewell Baptist Church, later called Hopewell Missionary Baptist Church, was founded about 1865 by Jack and Patsy Boyce and other African American families after they were freed from slavery. The original church building was lost to fire; this photograph shows one of the subsequent church buildings, faced with granite from Stone Mountain, some 10 miles away. (Courtesy of the Authors.)

The Lively House on South Peachtree Street in Norcross is named for Milton C. Lively (1820–1895), who together with his son-in-law, Stephen Tilly McElroy, moved from DeKalb County to Norcross and established a sawmill to serve the coming railroad. Lively and McElroy became founding fathers of Norcross and served together on the town's first city council. The house is thought to date from about 1835. (Courtesy of the Authors.)

John J. "Cousin John" Thrasher (1818–1899) purchased about 250 acres of land around the planned first stop on a new railroad north of Atlanta. Thrasher subdivided his land into smaller lots for a town and sold them at auction when the railroad arrived in 1870. He named the town for his good friend Jonathan Norcross. (Courtesy of David Sumner.)

Norcross was officially chartered on October 26, 1870, with the town limits stretching three quarters of a mile in every direction from the original depot, which is shown with cargoes of cotton bales and horse harnesses awaiting shipment. This building was situated south of what is today Holcomb Bridge Road. This depot was replaced in 1909. (Courtesy of Carl and Sherry Johnson.)

Jonathan Norcross (1808–1898) of Orono, Maine, moved to Marthasville, Georgia (present-day Atlanta), in 1845, and established a sawmill and a general merchandise store. In 1851, he became Atlanta's fourth mayor, and by then, had become good friends with fellow early Atlantan John Thrasher. Thrasher named the town of Norcross after him. Jonathan Norcross is shown on the left with fellow Atlanta pioneers Wash Collier (center) and George Adair in the 1890s. The site of what is now Atlanta was fixed in 1837, when Col. Stephen Long, who was charged with surveying the route of the state-owned Western & Atlantic Railroad, established the southern terminus of the railroad at a site within a few blocks of the state capitol building. Atlanta was called Terminus in its early years, and another name for it was Thrasherville, after John Thrasher. (Courtesy of the James G. Kenan Research Center at the Atlanta History Center.)

The Brunswick Hotel was built by John Thrasher and helped establish Norcross as a resort town. It was located at what is now the corner of Park Drive and Thrasher Street and featured 29 rooms and two stories (both with wraparound porches). The hotel went out of business during the Great Depression, and the building was demolished in the 1950s to make room for a post office. (Courtesy of Dr. James Woods.)

The first-floor porch at the Brunswick Hotel was quintessentially Southern—deep, with tall columns, plenty of shade, and comfortable, inviting rocking chairs. Here, guests could enjoy the afternoon listening to music from the concert band in the nearby park and review the arrival of trains, such as the daily Air Line Belle, which brought workers and visitors from Atlanta each evening. (Courtesy of Carl and Sherry Johnson.)

Pictured is the dinner bell that was salvaged from the Brunswick Hotel, which was razed in the 1950s. The December 1879 issue of *Harper's New Monthly Magazine* featured an article entitled "The City of Atlanta," in which John J. Thrasher was mentioned. The article also included a sketch of Thrasher enthusiastically ringing this bell. (Courtesy of Amelia Welch.)

In the late 1800s, there were three hotels in downtown Norcross: the Brunswick Hotel, the Martin Hotel, and the Medlock House, pictured in 1906. The Medlock House hotel was built by R.O. Medlock and was later demolished; part of the structure was moved to the southwest corner of Holcomb Bridge Road and Thrasher Street. That remaining remnant was subsequently replaced by a brick home. (Courtesy of Evelyn Nesbit Norman.)

The Norcross Methodist Church origins date to approximately 1818, when Medlock's Chapel was formed about one and a half miles southeast of what is now Norcross. Later, this church moved to a location on present-day North Norcross–Tucker Road and was renamed Flint Hill Methodist Church. This congregation moved to Norcross after 1870 and constructed this building in about 1875 on land purchased from John Thrasher and Milton C. Lively. In 1968, the church moved to Beaver Ruin Road. (Courtesy of Evelyn Nesbit Norman.)

Town founder John J. Thrasher and 16 others founded the Baptist Church of Christ in Norcross in 1872. For several years, this church held services in the Community House, which was also used by the Methodists and Presbyterians. The building shown in the photograph was completed in about 1884 and served the congregation until 1963, when it moved to a larger facility on North Peachtree Street. (Courtesy of Carl and Sherry Johnson.)

The Norcross Presbyterian Church traces its roots to 1833, when Goshen Presbyterian Church was established near the intersection of present-day Beaver Ruin and Hopkins Mill Roads. The church moved to Norcross after the town was founded and built the facility pictured in 1899, by which time it was known as the Norcross Presbyterian Church. The church moved to Medlock Bridge Road in 1965. (Courtesy of Carl and Sherry Johnson.)

The house at 297 South Peachtree Street is thought to be one of oldest homes in Norcross, perhaps predating 1870. Pictured at right is Parrie Hunt, aunt of early Norcross businessman R.O. Medlock, along with her sister and husband. In 1946, Ralph and Evelyn "Bud" Norman purchased the house. At the time this book was published, their family had lived in this house for more than 60 years. (Courtesy of Evelyn Nesbit Norman.)

Joel Chandler Harris (1845–1908) is pictured on the right with industrialist Andrew Carnegie. In the foreword to his second book of Uncle Remus stories, *Nights with Uncle Remus* (1883), Harris wrote that many of the stories in the book had come from an evening spent at the Norcross train depot. As he was waiting for a train there, he had an extended joint storytelling session with a group of black laborers. (Courtesy of the James G. Kenan Research Center at the Atlanta History Center.)

Buford Highway, completed through Norcross in 1937, was the first paved road into town. This house, on Buford Highway at South Pittman Circle, remained standing until the 1990s, when the land was developed for commercial use. George (1895–1985) and Ethel (1897–1986) Stevens lived here for many years, with several members of their extended family living in adjacent houses. (Courtesy of Al Karnitz.)

Two

NORCROSS AT WORK

Norcross's second railroad depot, shown shortly after it was built in 1909, replaced the original depot and was the center of the town's business activities for many years. The signs for "Whites Waiting Room" and "Colored Waiting Room" are indicative of the segregated facilities that were common in the southern United States at the time. (Courtesy of Carl and Sherry Johnson.)

Henry Johnson Reynolds (1871–1958), originally from Toccoa, is shown with an unidentified porter. Reynolds was a Southern Railroad conductor who lived in Norcross for many years. He was the senior conductor on the line at his retirement with 60 years of service, having worked for such illustrious passengers as presidents Herbert Hoover and Franklin D. Roosevelt. (Courtesy of Jack Reynolds.)

Jones C. Davenport (seated left), postmaster for the Southern Railroad, is pictured in his Atlanta office with his staff. The post office relied heavily on the railroads to move the nation's mail from city to city. As trains moved along, railroad workers used hooks to retrieve mailbags left hanging by the tracks for pickup while tossing bags of incoming mail to the platform. (Courtesy of Joyce Davenport Clark.)

Cotton was an important crop for farmers in the Norcross area from Civil War times until the wholesale invasion of the crop-destroying boll weevil in the early 1900s. In the fall, many local farmers brought their cotton crop to the Summerour Cotton Gin in Norcross (shown). Ginning the cotton separated the fiber from the seeds. This step was necessary before the cotton fiber could be processed into thread for cloth. The cotton gin, thought of as one of the key inventions of the Industrial Revolution, is generally credited to Eli Whitney, a native of Massachusetts who worked on the Georgia farmland owned by the widow of Revolutionary War hero Nathaniel Greene, Catharine "Caty" Littlefield Greene. Whitney had come south from New England to make his fortune and met Mrs. Greene during the trip. (Courtesy of Carl and Sherry Johnson.)

Local farmer Homer Summerour developed a new variety of cotton in the early 1900s; he called it Half and Half, implying that the cotton gave a 50 percent yield of fiber from the ginning process, a better result than was achieved with standard cotton seed available at the time. His son Ben (shown here with his wife Grady) ran the family's cotton ginning and farming operations for many years. (Courtesy of Skip Nau.)

Several employees from the B.F. Summerour Seed Company pose for a photograph while attending a meeting in Decatur, Georgia, around 1945. They include Mary Dean Scott (far left) and Ruby Grogan (third from left). Ben Summerour retired from the seed business and sold his farm to the Atlanta Athletic Club in the late 1960s; the property is a golf course today. (Courtesy of Betty Scott Jarrett.)

Unidentified workers weigh a large bale of cotton at the Summerour cotton gin complex on Lawrenceville Street. Although the gin is no longer in operation, the building still stands and is located behind the current city hall in Norcross. The term "gin" is an abbreviation for the word "engine." (Courtesy of Skip Nau.)

In 1885, A.A. Johnson and his cousin, A.A. Martin, opened a general store in Norcross at 15 Jones Street. Their partnership dissolved in 1889, but the store continued with Johnson and his descendants as proprietors, open for 103 years before it closed in 1988. At that time, it was the second oldest continuing business in Gwinnett County. (Courtesy of Carl and Sherry Johnson.)

For many years, Thomas E. Johnson Jr. (shown in his World War II Marines Corps uniform) ran Johnson's Store, which was started by his grandfather, A.A. Johnson. During his service in the war, Thomas was stationed in Iceland and earned the nickname "Pappy," because he was older than his fellow recruits. The name stuck, and he was called that by his grandchildren later in life. Like many in the Johnson family, Thomas was active in the Norcross Baptist Church and served for a time as a deacon there. He and his wife raised two children, Carl and Thomas "Edwin." As a storeowner and neighbor, Thomas Johnson was beloved by many in the community. When he died in 1988, several hundred people turned out for his funeral, at which he was memorialized with a 21-gun salute. (Courtesy of Michelle Morgan.)

The Bank of Norcross opened in February 1904 with S.T. McElroy as its first president and a board of directors composed of prominent local residents. Initially located at 19 South Peachtree Street, it moved in 1930 to the building pictured at the corner of South Peachtree and Jones Streets. It became part of the C&S banking system in 1967, and this branch was eventually closed. (Courtesy of Norcross High School.)

C.A. "Gus" McDaniel, shown, was cashier at the Bank of Norcross. In addition, he sold insurance, served as a deacon in the local Baptist church, and was mayor of the town. His wife, Maude Key McDaniel, was the daughter of Civil War veteran Dr. Thomas T. Key. (Courtesy of Norcross Masonic Lodge.)

Minor Pounds Garner is shown in front of Garner's Store, which he owned and operated for more than 40 years. He was active in many aspects of the community, including the First Methodist Church, the city council, the merchants association, the Masonic lodge, and the volunteer fire department. (Courtesy of Richard Garner.)

This receipt details a purchase in 1911 by the local Masons from "J.R. Garner, Dealer in Staple and Fancy Groceries." It appears that a celebration was planned for this summer day, as they purchased melons and ingredients for lemonade (sugar, lemons, and ice). Note the relatively high price of the lemons (which were shipped in from Florida) and that the phone number for the store was simply 5. (Courtesy of Norcross Masonic Lodge.)

Frank B. Nesbit came to Norcross as a young man to work with his grandfather Milton Lively and his wife's uncle S.T. McElroy. He became a partner in McElroy and Nesbit Furniture Company, located on Factory Street, off Carlyle Street. Nesbit spent much of his time in the mountains in Rabun County overseeing the cutting and shipping of lumber to the furniture factory in Norcross. (Courtesy of Evelyn Nesbit Norman.)

Sylvester Cain (1877–1948) and his wife, Maybelle (1878–1948), were active in a number of Norcross business ventures in the early 1900s and jointly ran the Brunswick Hotel after 1910. Maybelle is shown with unidentified associates at her dry goods store. They lived at 39 Thrasher Street. (Courtesy of Carl and Sherry Johnson.)

Shown about 1900, local entrepreneur Riley Owen "R.O." Medlock (center) was the owner of the brick building in the background. His Medlock Harness Company operated there and served an area covering several states. Years later, the first floor of this building was the home of Parson's grocery store. (Courtesy of Evelyn Nesbit Norman.)

Among the first in Gwinnett County to raise broilers for Gainesville businessman Jesse Jewell's booming poultry enterprise were three daughters of the local Jones family (Ruby Jones, Mattie Jones Wingo, and Eda Jones Thomas). Pictured in the 1940s are Ruby Jones (left) and Mattie Jones Wingo (with a chicken). Their family farm was located near Jones Bridge. (Courtesy of Michelle Morgan.)

Norcross businessman R.O. Medlock is pictured in his office in Atlanta with his stenographer. The office was in the Empire Building, one of the city's first skyscrapers. Medlock died there on June 25, 1909, when he accidentally fell several stories down an elevator shaft while on the way to his office. He was a successful entrepreneur and one of the largest owners of property, and source of taxes, in the Norcross area at the time of his death. The Empire Building, which was still standing at the time of this publication, is 10 stories and was the tallest building in the city of Atlanta from the time it was built in 1902 until 1906. It is located at 35 Broad Street, which is in the central downtown business district, near the current Richard Russell Federal Building. (Courtesy of Evelyn Nesbit Norman.)

Absalom Holbrook "A.H." Wingo (1859–1924) was a local physician and also a deacon at the First Baptist Church of Norcross. He was married twice, first to Nancy Alice Smith and then to Lula G. Sheek, fathering 10 children in all. His sons Ivey Wingo and Absalom "Red" Wingo played professional baseball. Wingo Street is named for his family. (Courtesy of Michelle Morgan.)

Dr. Ben Clement had a dental office in Norcross in the early 1900s and served one term as mayor. He was a large man and was frequently seen wearing his signature wide-brimmed hat, similar to a 10-gallon cowboy hat. He had a home in Norcross and a farm and country home near Cumming. In summers, he was sometimes seen coming from the farm in a mule-drawn buggy. (Courtesy of Danny Lay.)

In 1900, William Keady was traveling to Duluth, intending to open a drugstore there. But when his train stopped at the Norcross station, the bustling activity he saw changed his mind, and he established the business here. This advertisement was printed at the time of the grand opening of his store, which was the only drugstore in the area for many years. (Courtesy of Jane Holbrook.)

KEADY'S
NEW DRUG STORE!

To Open in Norcross
Saturday, December 1st.

A
Complete
NEW

STOCK
—OF—

DRUGS,

CHEMICALS,

PATENTS,

SODA
WATER,
STATIONERY,
FINE
CANDIES,
CIGARS
—AND—
TOBACCO.

Our Prescription department will be complete in all details, while every prescription will be compounded with the utmost of care.
Everything in our stock shall be furnished to our customers at Atlanta Prices.
We kindly solicit your patronage.

W. M. KEADY.

Charles Pinckney "Pink" Lively (1840–1926), pictured behind the counter of his store, was the son of one of the town's early settlers, Milton C. Lively. For a number of years, Pink, along with his son Henry M. "Doc" Lively, ran a retail store in downtown Norcross. C.P. Lively also served for a time on the Norcross City Council. (Courtesy of Carl and Sherry Johnson.)

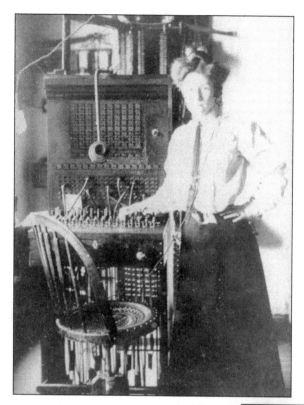

Norcross had a manually switched telephone exchange early in the 1900s; the switchboard was located in the home of Rev. Thomas Twitty on Railroad (now Wingo) Street. Reverend Twitty's daughter Floy (shown) was the main operator. Floy Twitty, one of 10 children, later married Frank "Poo-Doo" Robertson, who was a town baseball player and served as mayor of Norcross. (Courtesy of Carl and Sherry Johnson.)

Noye Nesbit, shown using a vintage telephone around 1980, recounted that, as a teenager, one of his jobs had been to spend his overnight hours at the telephone exchange to be ready for any important calls needing immediate attention during that time. Nesbit was born in Norcross and retired here after a career with Standard Oil. (Courtesy of Lillian Hicks Webb.)

In the early 1900s, several blacksmith shops, operated by John Adams, Hiram Terrell, and others, were located on Back Alley (today's Skin Alley). In this 1915 photograph, Terrell and his son Los are shoeing a horse belonging to Dr. Farmer Letson, a local physician. (Courtesy of Carl and Sherry Johnson.)

Christopher Columbus "Lum" Howell (1904–1965), a respected leader in the Norcross black community, operated a blacksmith shop on Skin Alley from the 1920s through the late 1950s. He had purchased the shop location from John Adams, another local smith. Property Howell owned on West Peachtree at Autry was later developed into the Lum Howell subdivision. (Courtesy of Carl and Sherry Johnson.)

Edward F. Buchanan, a local boy who was raised by foster parents, built on his exceptional talent as a telegraph operator and achieved millionaire status as a stockbroker in New York City in the early 1900s. Buchanan established Georgia's first automobile manufacturing company in Norcross—an advertisement for their Nor-X is pictured. In 1908, he lost his fortune in a trading scheme gone wrong. (Courtesy of Carl and Sherry Johnson.)

Hal Cofer lost his 80-acre farm on Rockbridge Road in the 1920s because of drought and the boll weevil. He subsequently moved into town, operating its only filling station for 32 years. Cofer was a Freemason for over 50 years, served as a Gwinnett County deputy sheriff, and was a skilled checker player, once earning the title of Gwinnett County Champion. (Courtesy of Thomas Ivy.)

George Verner (1897–1973) ran an auto repair shop in the 1930s on Jones Street behind the Bank of Norcross building. Robbie Burnett (left) and Red Gresham are shown at the shop. Up until this time, it was mainly the automobile owner's responsibility to make his own repairs. (Courtesy of Michelle Morgan.)

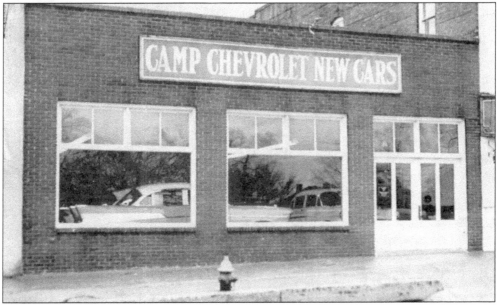

Camp Chevrolet dealership opened after World War II on South Peachtree Street in the center of downtown Norcross (shown) and remained on South Peachtree Street for about 10 years. The business moved from Norcross to Buford Highway in Chamblee, Georgia, and closed in the late 1970s. (Courtesy of Norcross High School.)

Carl Garner Sr.'s filling station opened on Buford Highway to serve the increasing amount of traffic on the road in the mid-1900s; it sold groceries and gas. Pictured in the foreground are Horace Minor (left) and Ben Scott (right); Willy Garmon is in the back. (Courtesy of Sandie Nesbit Speer.)

Betty Scott Jarrett is pictured in 1955 at the Swan Theater, located on the first floor of the Masonic Hall in the main block of South Peachtree Street. The Swan showed movies in the 1940s and 1950s and was operated by Bill Akin and later by the Zebell family. Prior to the opening of this business, the closest movie theater was in the Buckhead area of Atlanta. (Courtesy of Betty Scott Jarrett.)

In the late 1960s, Georgia Tech graduate Paul Duke (1924–2009) had a vision of a high-tech industrial and research park in then largely undeveloped southwestern Gwinnett County. He convinced 17 friends and business associates to invest with him to help turn that vision into a reality, resulting in Technology Park/Atlanta. (Courtesy of Elliott Brack.)

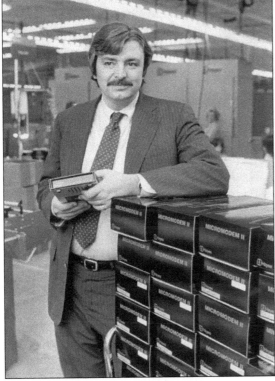

Dennis C. Hayes (shown) was one of the best-known entrepreneurs in the Technology Park/Atlanta development in the 1980s. His company, Hayes Microcomputer Products, was a pioneer in the manufacture of so-called smart modems, which were a major step toward the wired society of today. (Courtesy of Elliott Brack.)

Norcross resident Horace Simpson is pictured at his retirement celebration after 40 years of employment with Allis-Chalmers and its successor company, AGCO. In addition to his warehouse work, Simpson worked part-time for 15 years teaching roller-skating to Norcross youngsters at Playland's roller-skating rink. (Courtesy of Horace Simpson.)

Howard and Earl Webb started a company making the Duratite brand of wood dough and surfacing putty products in the 1920s, with manufacturing facilities in Norcross and in California. Many of their products were used to repair wooden boats. In this photograph, Howard Webb is standing on the right behind his brother Earl at a trade show. (Courtesy of Lillian Hicks Webb.)

Three

FAMILY AND
COMMUNITY LIFE

This wedding portrait of Jones C. Davenport (1866–1948) and Neppie Grogan Davenport (1872–1949) dates from 1895. Jones Davenport, who worked for the Southern Railroad, was born and raised in South Carolina. He met Neppie, a member of the Gwinnett pioneer Grogan family, while traveling and decided to move to Norcross to marry her; his father and other family members moved to Norcross with him. (Courtesy of Joyce Davenport Clark.)

The house at 319 South Peachtree Street was built about 1887 by W.C. Wall, a businessman who owned a general store and livery. It originally had four rooms with an outdoor kitchen and outdoor privy in the rear. In 1895, the house was purchased by Jones and Neppie Davenport, who twice added to it—in 1905 and again in 1915. (Courtesy of Joyce Davenport Clark.)

Mary Frances Stancil Grogan, Lina Grogan Waites, and Alice Waites are shown spinning thread on the back porch of the Davenport house around 1905. Walt Waites and his son are in the background. Spinning is historically an iconic home industry for women. This photograph demonstrates that thread spinning was still done at home by some Southern women as late as the beginning of the 20th century. (Courtesy of Joyce Davenport Clark.)

Ida Barkley Walker was a student at Spelman College in Atlanta when she met her future husband, Tom Walker, a farmer and storeowner in Norcross. The Walkers are pictured in 1916 with their two children, James Kenneth and Annie. Ida's parents disapproved strongly of their daughter's marriage to Tom Walker, believing that she had married beneath her station in life and had wasted her education by leaving the city to perform manual labor on a farm in the Norcross countryside. In 1918, Ida's parents, who had since moved from Atlanta to Baltimore, convinced her to join them in Baltimore, leaving Tom to raise their two children alone in Norcross. Ida died a few years later, at the age of 35, of a broken heart. Tom remained a widower for many years until marrying again later in his life. (Courtesy of Deborah Walker Little.)

James Kenneth Walker (far right) and family are shown on his father's porch in Norcross in 1952. Walker, while serving as a cook at a base in Mississippi during World War II, proved his skills in the kitchen one evening when he served chicken fricassee. A visiting high-ranking officer enjoyed it so much that he promoted Walker to the rank of sergeant on the spot. (Courtesy of Deborah Walker Little.)

Noel T. Knight (1930–1974) was the son of Norcross cotton broker Frank Knight and wife Barbara. The Knight family lived on Lively Avenue in a home with a lake on the property. Knight was a veteran of the Korean conflict. This photograph was taken at Arrowhead Camp in North Carolina in August 1942, after he had won a prize in a horse show. (Courtesy of Deborah Walker Little.)

This photograph, taken in 1942 at the home of Verne and Mae Nesbit on South Peachtree Street, shows Frank B. Nesbit (fourth row, third from left) with his six surviving sons (Noye, Maurice, Frank, Verne, Elwin, and Curtis) and other family members. Nesbit's wife, Frances, had died in 1937. (Courtesy of Jimmy Nesbit.)

Joseph Nesbit had this house built on a two-acre tract of land on North Peachtree Street about 1904. Nesbit was a conductor for Southern Railroad and the grandson of pioneer Gwinnett settler William Nesbit. He and his wife, Minnie, had five children and were known for their entertaining. Whenever Minnie Nesbit made a new dress, she and her husband had a party so that she could show it off. (Courtesy of Carl and Sherry Johnson.)

Pictured about 1950 on an outing to the big city of Atlanta are Annie Mae Dean Lay (left), her husband, James Chiles Lay, and their daughter Lynn. This photograph was taken on Peachtree Street in downtown Atlanta, outside Davison's department store. Annie Mae's father, Edwin "Pop" Dean, was a local railroad man and baseball talent scout for many years. The Dean family lived on Church Street in Norcross, which was the site of the original Community House that was used in the early years of the town by local churches and the Masonic Order. The name of the street was changed to Sunset Drive in the 1960s at the urging of some of the residents. The street was known unofficially as Holy Row for many years. Both James and Annie Mae Lay worked for the US Postal Service. (Courtesy of Danny Lay.)

Capt. Thomas Rainey (1866–1947) worked as a flagman and then conductor for the Southern Railroad and its predecessor companies for 53 years, retiring in 1937. He and his wife, Addie Brandon Rainey, raised five children and lived in this house on South Peachtree Street in Norcross for many years. (Courtesy of the Authors.)

Abraham Allen "A.A." Johnson (1853–1939) assumed responsibility for his family's Gwinnett County farm home when he was eight years old after the death of his father during the Civil War. He and his wife, Mary Hudson Johnson, moved in 1885 to Norcross, where he established a store and they raised a family of 12 children. A.A. served on the Norcross City Council. (Courtesy of Michelle Morgan.)

When their home on Barton Street was constructed, the Johnsons owned substantial property behind it between Sunset Drive and Holcomb Bridge Road. This land included Johnson's Lake, the site of fishing, boating, swimming, and baptismal ceremonies held by the nearby Norcross Baptist Church. (Courtesy of Carl and Sherry Johnson.)

Of A.A. and Mary Johnson's 12 children, most played at least one musical instrument. Shown is son Gus (1896–1948), who played the tuba in the "family band." A.A., Mary, son Gus, daughter Louette, and many other Johnson family members are buried in the Norcross City Cemetery. (Courtesy of Michelle Morgan.)

Louette Johnson Rochester (left), shown with her sisters Viola, Ruth, and Myrt (from left to right), was the daughter of A.A. and Mary Hudson Johnson. Some time after her husband's death, she built a house overlooking Thrasher Park at the corner of North Peachtree Street and Park Drive. She eventually sold this house to Winford Kent, who lived there for many years. (Courtesy of Michelle Morgan.)

This picture shows Dr. O.O. Simpson (1860–1943), third from left, his son Ollie (rear), and several other family members. Dr. Simpson graduated from Atlanta Medical College in 1882 and practiced medicine in Norcross for many years. He was elected mayor of Norcross twice and served on the Gwinnett County Commission and in the state legislature. (Courtesy of Jimmy Nesbit.)

Mattie Rakestraw Simpson (1870–1955), shown at right, was the third wife of Dr. O.O. Simpson and the mother of his eight children—two sons and six daughters. Lala Simpson Summerour (1871–1960), shown at left, was Dr. Simpson's youngest sister. The ladies are in front of the Nesbit house, which stood at the corner of Thrasher and Autry Streets for nearly 100 years until it was demolished around 1990. (Courtesy of Jimmy Nesbit.)

Benjamin Franklin "Frank" Simpson (1898–1939) and his wife, Vera Davenport Simpson, were high school sweethearts; they married after Frank finished his law degree at Atlanta Law School. The couple is shown on their honeymoon trip to Florida around 1925. Frank Simpson died at an early age because of a heart condition. (Courtesy of Joyce Davenport Clark.)

Martha Simpson was one of the twin girls (Martha and Sue) born to Ollie Simpson and Anne McClure Simpson in 1916. This photograph was taken in 1934 on the Chattahoochee River. She married Curtis Nesbit, and she obtained her teaching degree from Oglethorpe University when she was 40 years old. After teaching for some years, she became the first female assistant principal in Gwinnett County. (Courtesy of Jimmy Nesbit.)

Estelle "Stella" Reynolds (1877–1974) was born in Lula, Georgia, and married Henry Johnson Reynolds of Toccoa. They moved to Norcross around 1900 so that Henry could be closer to the start of his runs on the railroad, usually out of Atlanta. The Reynolds had six children, but one died at a young age. They raised their family in their home on Thrasher Street. (Courtesy of Jack Reynolds.)

Stella Reynolds (left) and Mary Hood Garner (right) were longtime members of the Norcross Woman's Club. They are pictured with Mrs. R.L. Rogers (center) of the Ninth District Federation of Women's Clubs during a luncheon honoring Reynolds for her 53 years of membership in the club. (Courtesy of Jimmy Garner.)

James Garner and his wife, Mary, moved to Norcross around 1908. His business, Garner's Store, offered live chickens (kept in coops to the side of the store) and fresh meat. Much of the livestock destined for the store was kept in pastures behind the family home on North Peachtree Street. (Courtesy of Jimmy Garner.)

This photograph of the children of James and Mary Lankford Garner includes, from left to right, Mary, Minor, Elsie, Raleigh, Lina, Robert Athel "At," and Carl Sr. Their sibling Richard Curtis Garner died as a child. Elsie and Lina were schoolteachers in Norcross, while At Garner was in the first group of draftees from Gwinnett County for World War I in 1917. (Courtesy of Richard Garner.)

This classic American Foursquare house was built during the early 1900s by Huss Beutell, who purchased a nine-acre site in 1892 from the Rakestraw family. Beutell's home featured modern conveniences (for the time), including running water provided by a privately owned water tower and supply lines. The Garner family purchased the home in 1930, owning it for the next 59 years. (Courtesy of Richard Garner.)

Lorenzo D. "Dutch" Ewing and Lottie Burnett Ewing grew up together in Norcross and married on June 23, 1923. Dutch worked for the Matthews Furniture Company and later served on the Lake Lanier Islands Development Authority and on the Norcross City Council. Lottie pursued a banking career, working for the Bank of Norcross, Atlanta Federal Reserve Bank, and the First National Bank of Atlanta. (Courtesy of Billy and Joann Weathers.)

This hilltop home on North Peachtree Street was originally owned by Norcross businessman Thompson "Tom" Ray. He was president of the Southern Oak Harness and Leather Company and ran the first dairy to serve the residents of Norcross. Ray and many members of his family are buried in the Norcross City Cemetery. (Courtesy of the Authors.)

Pictured is the monument marking the grave of Marion Wesley Ray (1871–1944). Ray and his wife, Lillie (1867–1946), were sharecroppers who worked for Marion's brother Thompson for many years. Wesley kept a diary that detailed many aspects of life in Norcross and travel in Georgia around the beginning of the 20th century. (Courtesy of the Authors.)

Frances Newton (right) and her daughter Ann Newton Barker (left) come from a family that has been active in the Hopewell Missionary Baptist Church for several generations. At the time this book was written, Frances, age 89, was the eldest African American Norcross native. In the early 1980s, Norcross city clerk Betty Mauldin hired Frances's daughter Ann, making her the city's first female African American employee. (Courtesy of Ann Newton Barker.)

Homer Virgil Jones (1858–1920) carried on the farming tradition of his father, Thomas Hardaway Jones, and worked for the Southern Railroad for many years. He was a founder of the Bank of Norcross and a Freemason and Shriner. While working for the Southern Railroad, he encountered three men robbing a railroad mail car and managed to apprehend one of the robbers while sustaining injuries that caused him to miss several weeks of work. He received a reward of $250 from the federal government for catching the robber. In 1907, Jones and his wife, Mollie James Jones, made a trip to New York City, which resulted in a $2,500 donation from Edward Buchanan to construct the library building in Norcross. Jones died at age 62 after a lengthy bout with Parkinson's disease (Courtesy of Jimmy Garner.)

Woman's Club members pose during the General Federation of Women's Clubs Golden Jubilee Triennial meeting in Atlantic City in 1941. From left to right are Mollie Jones, Stella Reynolds (both of Norcross), and Mrs. Pinson (of Baconton, Georgia). At the time, Stella Reynolds was the president of the Ninth District Federation of Woman's Clubs and chaired the United Service Organizations (USO) fundraising efforts in Norcross. (Courtesy of Jack Reynolds and Amelia Welch.)

The three young Norcross girls shown are, from left to right, Annie, Betty, and Florence Thompson. They were the daughters of Gene and Slety Thompson, and the photograph dates from the 1930s. As adults, all three women married, becoming Annie Bailey, Betty Warbington, and Florence Grogan. (Courtesy of Rufus Dunnigan.)

John Adams and his bride, Amanda, moved to Norcross in 1896. Adams was a blacksmith in the Norcross area for the next 40 years, part of the time from a shop on Back (Skin) Alley. This picture shows the couple around 1908 with their four children, who are, from left to right, Noah, Worley, Carrie Lou, and Winnie. (Courtesy of John Adams.)

Arch and Lucy Adams Hamilton, shown in their cornfield, were sharecroppers who farmed land that is now part of the Peachtree Memorial Park Cemetery on Peachtree Industrial Boulevard. The old farmhouse still stands on that property. Lucy Adams Hamilton was the daughter of Norcross blacksmith John Adams and his wife, Amanda Adams. (Courtesy of Lynn Hamilton Griffeth.)

Cleo Hamilton stands in front of a large car on Jones Bridge, a single-lane bridge with a wooden-plank deck that connected Gwinnett and Milton (later Fulton) Counties. There was a ferry at this location before the bridge was built in 1904. Jones Bridge fell into disrepair around 1940 and was partially dismantled during World War II. (Courtesy of Lynn Hamilton Griffeth.)

Most Norcross residents in the early 20th century had their own gardens, and a familiar sight was local farmer Hardy Strickland and his mule tilling many of those gardens at the beginning and end of the growing season. He is pictured with young Jack Reynolds Jr., who is sitting atop of Strickland's mule about 1952. (Courtesy of Jack Reynolds.)

The Depot Gang was a group of young Norcross men who came of age in the late 1950s. Members included future civic and business leaders such as Dodger DeLeon and Carl Garner Jr. They got their name from their habit of riding their hot rods down to the depot in Norcross to hang out; they were also rumored to drag race through Pinckneyville. (Courtesy of Dodger DeLeon.)

The Norcross Open Car show was begun in 1997 by Depot Gang members as a fundraising event to help defray the medical expenses of Kristi DeLeon, a local nursing student who was critically injured in an automobile accident. DeLeon died of her injuries, but her memory lives on in the annual car show, which has raised over $200,000 for nursing and medical scholarships. Pictured are recent scholarship winners. (Courtesy of Dodger DeLeon.)

Jimmy Carlyle, the nephew of baseball standout Roy Carlyle, grew up in Norcross and served as postmaster for a number of years. As a young boy, one of his favorite companions was his pet goat Filbert (shown). Roy Carlyle lived in Norcross after his retirement from baseball and ran a hardware store. (Courtesy of Julie Rutkowski.)

Dodger DeLeon grew up on Norcross Tucker Road and is shown with his lifelong friend Lawrence Harris and his pet goat Marvin. Dodger recalls vividly the level of unhappiness that his mother displayed when she returned home one day to find her son and Marvin together in the kitchen eating peanut butter! (Courtesy of Dodger DeLeon.)

63

Florence Warbington Green grew up in the rock-faced house on Holcomb Bridge at Barton Street and graduated from Norcross High School in 1940. She was active in the Norcross Garden Club and was a well-respected local artist. She participated in the Piedmont Arts Festival and won a statewide prize from the Georgia Woman's Clubs in the early 1970s. Her painting of downtown Norcross hangs in city hall. (Courtesy of Michelle Morgan.)

The Buchanan House, pictured after a snowstorm in 1939, sits at the north corner of Thrasher Park. Completed in 1907, it was built by Edward F. Buchanan for his foster parents, was later used as a hospital by Dr. Nim Guthrie, and was then the residence of Frank and Vera Simpson. (Courtesy of Carl and Sherry Johnson.)

The Medlock family traces its roots in Gwinnett County back to Isham Medlock (1775–1852). Isham was listed as a pioneer in Gwinnett County in 1818, having come from Jackson County. Isham's grandson Robert Medlock was the third generation of Medlocks to live in Gwinnett County. Medlock Bridge and Medlock Bridge Road north of Norcross are named for Robert's son William Oliver Nesbit Medlock, who operated a ferry and built the first bridge at this location. During the latter part of his life, Robert lived in the house that is pictured. This home was the site of the annual Medlock reunion as well as the Pinckneyville Spring Festival. Taken at a Medlock family reunion at the Medlock house (previously standing near the intersection of Spalding Drive and Holcomb Bridge Road) during the 1970s, this photograph shows the extent of the family's growth in Gwinnett over the last 150-plus years. (Courtesy of Lori Medlock Anderson.)

Jewel Parsons (in the white coat) waits at the Norcross railroad depot with her children (from left to right) Joe, John, and Jane to catch the approaching train. Her husband, Jack, ran Parson's Store in downtown Norcross for many years in the mid-20th century. Parson's Store was located at the corner of Jones and Railroad (now Wingo) Streets. (Courtesy of Charles Carroll.)

The Norcross Concert Band, shown at the Norcross High School, was an active part of community life in the early 1900s, performing regularly in the city park. It also performed in more distant venues, such as the 1907 Jamestown Tercentennial Exhibition in Virginia. Carl Wootten, a band member, used his experience in Norcross to later get a job with the band led by the famous "March King," John Philip Sousa. (Courtesy of Ken Weatherford.)

Ollie Ivey is pictured (front left) at a gathering with her friends at the popular picnic spot near Jones Bridge on the Chattahoochee River. The photograph dates from early in the 20th century. Jones Bridge County Park opened in the 1970s, and it remains a favorite gathering place. (Courtesy of Lynn Hamilton Griffeth.)

The family of E. Winn Born, a prominent lawyer who served as mayor of Norcross, built this house in the 1880s on Born Street at Wingo Street. Tom and Lessie Lawson Ivy bought the house in 1940, and their family owned the home until Lessie passed away in 1987. The house was used as a location during filming of the low-budget comedy movie *Fast Food* around 1988. (Courtesy of Thomas Ivy.)

Edgar Lafayette Ivy was the great-grandson of Hardy Ivy, one of the first settlers in today's Atlanta. Edgar and his wife, Sally Howell Ivy, raised seven children on their farm near the intersection of today's South Old Peachtree Road and Peachtree Industrial Boulevard. They are shown with their youngest son, Royal Howell "Red" Ivy, working on their property around 1930. Hardy Ivy died from an accident prior to 1850, but his wife, Sarah, lived a number of years afterwards and is buried in Oakland Cemetery in Atlanta along with other members of her family. There was an Ivy Street in downtown Atlanta for many years, but the city changed the name of the street to Peachtree Center Boulevard in the latter part of the 20th century. Hardy and Sarah Ivy had a large family, and one of their sons is buried in the cemetery at Mount Carmel Methodist Church near Norcross. (Courtesy of Thomas Ivy.)

Four

CHURCHES, SCHOOLS, AND ORGANIZATIONS

In the 1930s, Shiloh Baptist Church on Spalding Drive held baptisms at the pool behind the stone home of Anderson Warbington on Holcomb Bridge Road at its intersection with Barton Street in Norcross. This photograph, dating from such an occasion in 1938, shows in the water, from left to right, Claude Benson, Mary Singleton Kelley, Bobbie Jennings, Mary Mullinax, Grace Robbs, and Rev. Avery Graves. (Courtesy of Annette Kelly Kellett.)

Under the leadership of its senior pastor, Bishop William L. Sheals, Hopewell Missionary Baptist Church has grown from a small, local historic church to a megachurch in the metro Atlanta area with 15,000 members. Its 2,500-seat sanctuary is topped by a spire with a gold cross, the highest cross (in elevation) in Gwinnett County. Construction of the sanctuary revitalized the area, replacing a junkyard. (Courtesy of the Authors.)

Rev. Willis Leander Jones, DD (1859–1913), is buried in the Hopewell Church cemetery. Jones grew up in Norcross and was of Native American and African descent. He was a founder of the Beulah Baptist Church on Griffin Street in Atlanta and served as pastor of the First African Baptist Church in Savannah, Georgia, from 1909 until his death. (Courtesy of the Authors.)

Pictured about 1970 after a service at the old sanctuary of Hopewell Missionary Baptist Church are, from left to right, Elmira Gamage, Frances Wheeler Sims, and Barbara Dunnigan. Elmira's husband, Richard Gamage, was pastor at Hopewell from 1970 to 1979. Hopewell Missionary Baptist Church was established by former slaves about 1865, around the time the Civil War ended. (Courtesy of Rufus Dunnigan.)

In 1980, Rufus Dunnigan (left) and Fred Simpson (right), two longtime members of Hopewell Missionary Baptist Church (shown with Fred's wife, Jeanette Newton Simpson), convinced William L. Sheals, then director of Public Housing in Atlanta and a part-time preacher at Mount Vernon Baptist Church, to become Hopewell's new pastor. At the time of publication, Reverend Sheals had been at Hopewell for over 30 years. (Courtesy of Ann Newton Barker.)

The land for Norcross City Cemetery was donated by pioneer settler Milton C. Lively at the time of the city's founding in 1870, and it is the final resting place of several hundred Norcross-area residents. This photograph, thought to date from the 1940s, shows the Methodist church in the distance (upper left) and the city water tower beyond that. (Courtesy of Jimmy Nesbit.)

In 1934, members of a Norcross Methodist Church fellowship group called the Epworth Pioneers built a log cabin behind the Methodist church. The church's youth group routinely met there, and 40 years later, Bill Curry, future football coach at Georgia Tech and other schools, taught there. (Courtesy of Norcross United Methodist Church.)

Mount Carmel Methodist Church, organized in 1828, is located on South Old Peachtree Road, two and a half miles north of Norcross. This area was in the center of the Pinckneyville settlement, and South Old Peachtree Road was part of the original Peachtree Road laid out by pioneer settler William Nesbit during the War of 1812. This photograph from about 1925 shows construction of the current brick church building. Previously, the church had met in two wooden buildings that were constructed in the 1800s. At the time of the construction of this building, there were substantial droughts in the Norcross area that made farm work unproductive. Many of the families attending the church were farmers, so some of them used their slack time to rebuild the church. Later in the 20th century, the church added on to the brick building to accommodate the growing congregation. (Courtesy of Lynn Hamilton Griffeth.)

Rev. S.F. Dowis was the pastor at the Norcross Baptist Church from 1919 to 1923. He is remembered for leading successful revivals and for his thundering preaching style. Dowis's brother Victor was a Gwinnett deputy sheriff who was involved in a controversial shooting of alleged bootleggers in 1922 and was murdered several months later. (Courtesy of Norcross Baptist Church.)

Rev. Thomas T. Twitty was the pastor at the Norcross Baptist Church from 1895 to 1904 and lived in Norcross on what is now called Wingo Street with his large family. He was the visiting preacher leading a revival in Gainesville in the summer of 1919 when, having just finished a sermon, he collapsed in the pulpit; a few minutes later, he was dead. (Courtesy of Norcross Baptist Church.)

This photograph from the early 1900s of four unidentified young ladies was taken at Mount Carmel Methodist Church Cemetery, one of the oldest cemeteries in the Norcross area. The cemetery dates from the time of the church's establishment in the late 1820s. There are several hundred people buried there, including veterans of wars dating from the early 1800s. A child of Hardy Ivy is buried here, as are many members of the Simpson, Medlock, and other families. Harold Medlock, who was the unofficial historian of the Pinckneyville community for many years and a member of the church, was buried here after his death in 2005 at age 76. He served in the US Army during the Korean Conflict and was awarded the Purple Heart and several other medals for his service. (Courtesy of Lori Medlock Anderson.)

Peter Marshall (1902–1949) was born in Scotland and came to America at age 24. While studying for the ministry in the late 1920s at the Columbia Theological Seminary in Atlanta, he served as the pastor at the Norcross Presbyterian Church. In the 1940s, he became well known during his service as US Senate chaplain. (Courtesy of Norcross Presbyterian Church.)

From left to right, Ruth Wingo, Annie Humphries, Ethel Sparks, and Sadie Simpson are pictured with Professor Bell at their 1911 graduation from Norcross High School. Sadie Simpson, one of Dr. O.O. Simpson's six daughters, later married John Howard Webb of Alpharetta. They settled in Norcross and had three children, Claire, Doris, and John "Jack Jr." Howard. (Courtesy of Joann and Billy Weathers.)

Ellen Mackey "Nelle" Jones (1898–1996) was great-granddaughter of Thomas Hardaway Jones and daughter of Louisa Brandon Burtchaell Jones and Reps Hardaway Jones. Jones devoted 49 years of her life to teaching. She taught at Glover Elementary School near Norcross and afterwards spent 29 years teaching in the Atlanta schools. Later, she was involved in shaping teaching programs in the Gwinnett County schools. At 68, Jones retired from teaching sixth grade at Summerour Elementary School. (Courtesy of Michelle Morgan.)

This photograph shows the members of the Norcross High School graduating class of 1930. Despite the event occurring in the early years of the Great Depression, these young men and women, in fancy dress, reflect great optimism on their graduation day. Seated at far left is Carrie Sue Westbrook, who would later marry Grady Simpson, longtime town police chief. (Courtesy of Carl and Sherry Johnson.)

Like so many schools in the South, Norcross schools were segregated by race until integration in the 1960s. The school for African American children in Norcross, known by the community as "the Schoolhouse," was located on Autry Street where Rossie Brundage Park is currently located. There were four rooms in the school: two rooms for the first through sixth graders and two rooms for the seventh through ninth grades. At the time this photograph was taken, students could only go as far as grade nine here; those who wanted to continue on to high school had to attend Booker T. Washington High in Atlanta. This building was used by the African American community as a gathering place as well as an educational institution. The school closed after 1955, when a school consolidation effort began in Gwinnett County and African American children attended consolidated schools in nearby cities. Students of all grades are pictured in front of the Schoolhouse. (Courtesy of Deborah Walker Little.)

When this photograph was taken in 1939, most schools in the southern United States were segregated by race. Pictured here are students with teacher Joann Parks at what was known as the Norcross Colored School on Autry Street (now the site of Rossie Brundage Park). Ernest Trimble was the school's principal. (Courtesy of Rufus Dunnigan.)

The Norcross High School building was erected by the city on College Street at Jones Street with the proceeds of bonds issued by the city in 1903. Because of its location and design, it was affectionately known as the "Castle on the Hill." The last high school class from this Norcross High School graduated in 1957. The building was demolished after some years of use as an elementary school. (Courtesy of Charles Carroll.)

In the mid-1950s, Gwinnett County's white and black schools underwent consolidation efforts. As a result, African American students from Norcross, Suwanee, Duluth, and Buggtown (a former slave community) were consolidated into two schools—Hooper Renwick High School in Lawrenceville and Hull Elementary in Duluth. Pictured is Harold Dunnigan in his 1959 Hull Elementary School photograph. (Courtesy of Rufus Dunnigan.)

School consolidation in 1957 had eliminated smaller high schools in southwestern Gwinnett in favor of the newly built West Gwinnett High School, located across Buford Highway from downtown Norcross. A few years later, West Gwinnett High was renamed Norcross High School; this photograph shows the first graduating class from the newly renamed school. (Courtesy of Norcross High School.)

Gwinnett County schools, along with many of the public school systems in the southern United States, were integrated in the mid-1960s. This photograph, taken at Cemetery Field in Norcross, shows the high school girls' softball team in 1970. Norcross High School has a long tradition of sports excellence from winning baseball championships in the mid-20th century to basketball and other sports. (Courtesy of Julie Rutkowski.)

Birdie Burnett Morton (1902–1964) was known affectionately by her students as "Miss Birdie." Morton graduated from Norcross schools and attended the State Normal School of Athens, Georgia, before a three-year teaching stint back in Norcross. She then attended Knoxville University, Asheville Normal School, and the Baptist Woman's Union Trading School in Louisville, Kentucky, before returning to Norcross to teach. A devoted first-grade teacher, Morton retired in 1962 after a 40-year career. (Courtesy of Billy and Joann Weathers.)

"Miss Ludie" Simpson (1877–1975), a longtime teacher in the Gwinnett County school system, inherited a large holding of land along the Chattahoochee River near the current Jones Bridge Park. Prior to her death, she arranged to transfer this land to the Methodist Church. This facility is known today as Simpsonwood, a 227-acre retreat and conference center. (Courtesy of Norcross High School.)

Ruth Jackson Davenport (1913–2007) was born in Milledgeville, Georgia, and graduated from Georgia State College for Women in 1934. She taught school in Norcross for almost 40 years, retiring in 1973. She married Jones Arnold "Cree" Davenport (1899–1978) and was a longtime member of the Norcross Woman's Club, the Norcross Garden Club, and the Norcross Methodist Church. She is pictured (top row, far right) with her 1953 class. (Courtesy of Betty Scott Jarrett.)

This photograph shows Norcross student Jack Reynolds in his school band uniform in the 1960s, a few years after the high school band was formed under the leadership of Georgette Clark. The band went on European tours from 1971 to 1974 under the leadership of John David Mardis and Logan Turrentine. (Courtesy of Jack Reynolds.)

Norcross Elementary School introduced tap dance classes to students in the 1950s as an after-school extracurricular activity. Practices at times were held at the home of librarian Emily Cook. Each year, the students who took tap lessons performed in a dance recital, and this photograph is from the 1955 recital. (Courtesy of Lynn Hamilton Griffeth.)

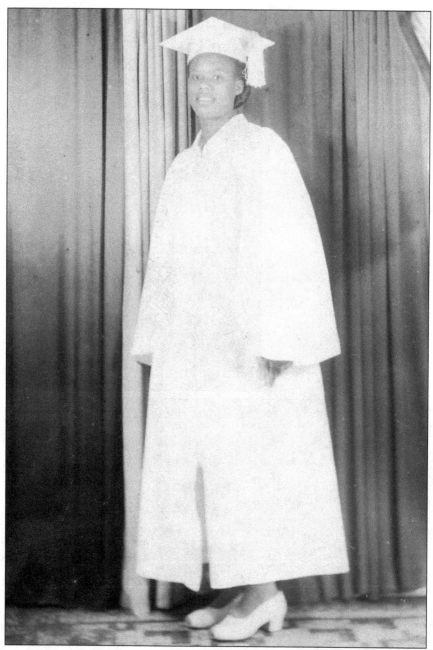

Cora Dunnigan was the daughter of Esters and Annie Lee Dunnigan. She is pictured in 1946 as she graduated from the prestigious Poro Beauty College, located on Auburn Avenue in Atlanta. Poro Beauty College was the brainchild of Annie M. Malone, who opened the first Poro College in Chicago, Illinois. Ella Martin, a protégé of Malone's, opened her branch of Poro in Atlanta in 1930 with Malone's blessing and backing. After graduation, Cora Dunnigan worked as a beautician. However, her career would change before long, as she set her sights on becoming a nurse. She returned to school, this time attending Beaumont Nursing School in Atlanta. When she graduated with her nursing degree, Dunnigan pursued a career in the medical field and enjoyed a successful career as a nurse specializing in private home care cases. (Courtesy of Rufus Dunnigan.)

The Norcross Woman's Club was formed in 1905, and it established Gwinnett County's first public library in Norcross on July 1, 1907. It was located in a small room in the public schoolhouse and moved several times before finding a long-term home at this building (the current site of the Norcross Woman's Club), which opened in 1921 with Lola Key as librarian. The library building's primary benefactor was Edward F. Buchanan. (Courtesy of the Authors.)

Betty Rochester Wingo (1924–1994), seated far left, was the Norcross librarian for many years. The library was located on North Peachtree Street for approximately 50 years (1921–1971) before it moved to a larger, more modern building on Carlyle Street to better accommodate the growing needs of the community. (Courtesy of Michelle Morgan.)

In 1957, the Norcross Public Library joined what became the Lake Lanier Regional Library, which served Gwinnett and Forsyth Counties. Pictured with the Lake Lanier Regional Library Bookmobile are Leon Maloney (mayor of Norcross), L.D. Strickland (superintendent of Summerour Middle School), Dutch Ewing, Lottie Ewing, Mary Jones, Col. Clifford Jones, and Mary Hood Garner of the Norcross Woman's Club. (Courtesy of Jimmy Garner.)

The Boy Scouts have been active in Norcross since at least the 1920s, when the Norcross Baptist Church sponsored a troop. The Cub Scout Pack 248 gathering, pictured in 1953, features local school board member and scoutmaster Bill Everett (in Indian headdress on the back row). (Courtesy of Danny Lay.)

Five

SPORTS AND RECREATION

Baseball was the most popular sport in Norcross for many years, starting in the early 20th century. Taken in August 1910, this photograph of the Norcross baseball team includes, from left to right, (first row) Carl Garner, Almon Grisson, Ollie Simpson, and Garland Terrell; (second row) Hugh Twitty, Herb Eason, Blount Burchelle, Los Terrell, and Frank "Poo-Doo" Robertson. (Courtesy of the Norcross Old Timers Baseball Association.)

Ivey Brown Wingo (1890–1941), pictured, spent his teen years playing baseball in Norcross. He was one of the many children in the family of pioneer Norcross physician Dr. A.H. Wingo. (Wingo Street is named for the family.) After minor-league assignments, Ivey joined the St. Louis Cardinals and then the Cincinnati Reds, where he played catcher until 1925. He caught three games for the Reds during the 1919 World Series against the White Sox, infamous for its so-called Black Sox gambling scandal. He returned to his hometown of Norcross when he retired holding the National League record for most games caught during a career, totaling 1,233 games. At one time, he also held the record for the most errors by a catcher during a career. Wingo died at an early age and is buried in the Norcross City Cemetery. (Courtesy of William M. Smith.)

Absalom Holbrook "Red" Wingo (on right
in the photograph, shown with his brother
Ivey) was a high-batting-average outfielder
for the Detroit Tigers in the 1920s after
working his way up from a start on the
Norcross town team. He worked for Ford
Motor Company in Detroit after his playing
days were over, but he was seen visiting
Norcross occasionally in his later life.
(Courtesy of Carl and Sherry Johnson.)

Roy Edward Carlyle began his
professional baseball career in 1922.
By 1927, he was playing outfield
for the New York Yankees during
a pennant-winning season. Carlyle
holds the record for the longest-
hit home run, a distance of 618
feet, which he hit in Oakland
Park, California. He retired to
his hometown of Norcross, where
he operated a hardware store
prior to his death in the 1950s.
(Courtesy of Julie Rutkowski.)

Wyatt "Mike" Davenport (1901–1922), son of Jones and Neppie Davenport of Norcross, was playing in a baseball game for Georgia Military College against Georgia Tech in the spring of 1922 when he and a fellow player collided while trying to catch a fly ball. Davenport died a few days after from the injuries sustained in the collision. The school later named its athletic field in his memory. (Courtesy of Joyce Davenport Clark.)

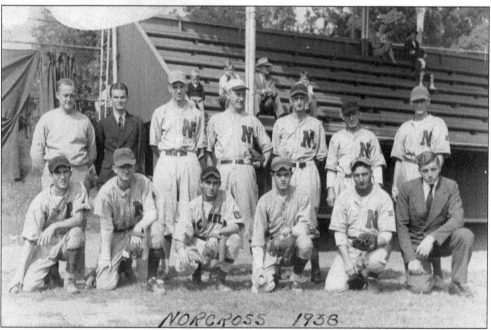

Pictured on October 2, 1938, is the Norcross town baseball team, champions of the Granite League. From left to right are (first row) Royce Cofer, Oliver Kelly, Troyce Cofer, John Adams, Horace Bishop, and Eugene Green; (second row) Howard Lietch, John Kelly, Hudson Johnson, Jack Reynolds, Joe "Pink" Nesbit, Bill Davenport, and Frank Moulder. (Courtesy of Jack Reynolds.)

In a scene reminiscent of Hal Roach's *Our Gang* series of the pre–World War II era, this photograph captures the Norcross sandlot baseball team champions from 1925. The body language depicted by practically each player in this photograph demonstrates the confidence and ability of these young champions. Sandlot-league baseball provided younger boys the opportunity to participate in league baseball play and was a precursor to today's Dixie Youth or Little League organizations. Several of these adolescent youths would feed their love of baseball by continuing their play as young men in local, college, and regional teams. From left to right are (first row) Jack Reynolds, Minor Garner, Harold Martin, Harry Myers, Jim Barrow, and George Mills; (second row) Claude Ball, Hollis Rochester, Joe "Pink" Nesbit, Harold Carlyle, Cecil Rhodes, and Joe S. Nesbit (coach). (Courtesy of Jack Reynolds.)

Jack "Shep" Trimble was a skilled baseball player with Norcross's black baseball team before taking his talents to the Atlanta Black Crackers, where he played in the 1930s and 1940s. After military service and his retirement from baseball, he returned to Norcross and taught youngsters the sport at Rossie Brundage Park. His brother Ernest was a school principal. (Courtesy of the Norcross Old Timers Baseball Association.)

This photograph shows Bill Payne (center) with Norcross baseball player Clint Davis (right), receiving the Georgia State Baseball Championship trophy for 1961 from an unidentified person. Payne was the manager of the highly successful Norcross town baseball team in the 1950s and 1960s. Under his leadership, the team won several league championships and played in three National Amateur Baseball Federation Tournaments (1961, 1964, and 1965). (Courtesy of Carl Garner Jr.)

This photograph pictures Edwin "Pop" Dean (1901–1964) with Norcross baseball players Robert Burnett (center) and Harold Ivy (right). As a youth, Dean was a baseball player, and as an adult, he continued his love for the game, organizing local teams and managing Norcross's American Legion team, which allowed play through age 17. Over the years, he coached strong teams and led them to several state championships. Dean had a very good relationship with Earl Mann, who owned the Atlanta Crackers, the predecessor team to the Atlanta Braves; therefore, he could arrange for Norcross boys to get tryouts with the Atlanta team, helping many players pursue their diamond dreams in local and regional leagues. This group included Harold Ivy, who played for the Atlanta Crackers. Pop Dean was also a reserve umpire for the old Southern Association League and would substitute umpiring at Atlanta Crackers games when called upon. (Courtesy of Louise Ivy Clark.)

On July 4, 2003, the Norcross Baseball Club honored its past with an Old Timers Day Tribute at the site of the old ball ground, which was constructed decades earlier. In 2010, the ball ground was converted into a park named in honor of longtime Norcross mayor Lillian Webb. (Courtesy of the Norcross Old Timers Baseball Association.)

For a number of years, the Atlanta Braves had a Norcross Night each year at their Atlanta–Fulton County Stadium home. This photograph shows Lillian Webb throwing out the first baseball at such an event during one of her early terms as mayor of the city. The Braves moved from Milwaukee, Wisconsin, to Atlanta in 1966. (Courtesy of Lillian Hicks Webb.)

A group of 12 young men from Norcross met at Carlyle Hardware Store in 1939 and paid $10 each to fund construction of a cabin on an island in the Chattahoochee River near Jones Bridge on land leased from Floyd McRae. However, flooding of the Chattahoochee River in the 1950s reduced the clubhouse to a pile of ruined boards, and their River Rats club was never reactivated. (Courtesy of Richard Garner.)

This photograph of three men on a fishing expedition was taken in 1952. Sitting in the jeep are Bill Anderson (behind the wheel) and Richard Garner. Victor Anderson is outside the jeep holding a minnow bucket. The Andersons came to visit their friend in Norcross so they could all go fishing at a lake on West Jones Bridge Circle. (Courtesy of Richard Garner.)

Pictured is Horace Simpson with his impressive fishing catch of the day, a large snapping turtle. Horace's friends cooked up the turtle, frying some of it and using other parts to make soup, which the group enjoyed later under a large oak tree. This photograph was taken in the driveway of Horace's West Peachtree Street home. This property once belonged to Norcross physician Dr. O.O. Simpson. (Courtesy of Horace Simpson.)

Cecil Simpson Carroll (1909–1999) and her eldest son, Harry Lee, are returning from a successful rabbit hunt in the snow-covered fields around Norcross in this photograph, taken about 1950. Cecil was the sister of longtime police chief Grady Simpson and the owner of a dairy in the Norcross area for 20 years. She also worked for the State of Georgia. (Courtesy of Richard Garner.)

Six

OUR MILITARY HERITAGE

During World War I, the Camp Gordon training base was at the current site of DeKalb Peachtree Airport in Chamblee, Georgia. The rifle range for the base was in Norcross (now the Sheffield Forest subdivision). Troops marched out from Chamblee and camped in tents at the rifle range (shown) while doing their target practice drills. World War I sharpshooting hero Sgt. Alvin York of Tennessee trained in Norcross. (Courtesy of Bob Basford.)

Many Confederate veterans in the Norcross area joined the Lovick Thomas Chapter of the United Confederate Veterans after the Civil War. Several Norcross-area men are pictured at one of their gatherings. Lovick Thomas was the captain of Company A of the 42nd Regiment of the Georgia Volunteer Infantry during the war; the company was nicknamed the "Gwinnett Beauregards." (Courtesy of Evelyn Nesbit Norman.)

William Daly Burtchaell (1834–1919) was born in Ireland and immigrated to Florida in the 1850s. He served in Robert E. Lee's Army of Northern Virginia during the Civil War. In the late 1800s, he built a large home called Holyoke (no longer standing), located near the intersection of Medlock Bridge Road and the current Peachtree Parkway. (Courtesy of Michelle Morgan.)

Paul T. Settle (1892–1918), of Norcross, served as a lieutenant in the US Army in World War I. As noted on this monument at his grave in the Norcross City Cemetery, he fought in the Meuse-Argonne campaign in the fall of 1918, was wounded in battle, and died three days after the armistice was signed on November 11, 1918. (Courtesy of the Authors.)

Noye Nesbit (1894–1989), of Norcross, worked his way through Georgia Tech and played football there for two years under coach John Heisman. This photograph shows Noye shortly after his graduation, when he was about to ship out to France for World War I service with the first antiaircraft unit in the American Expeditionary Force. (Courtesy of the Georgia Tech Foundation's *Images and Memories Photograph Collection* [1985].)

Carl Andrew Garner Sr. (1893–1977), third from left, served in the Marines during World War I and is pictured in 1917 at training camp in Parris Island, South Carolina. Garner later served as mayor of Norcross and on the city council. He married local schoolteacher Mary Hood Garner (1903–1977) in 1930, and they had two sons. (Courtesy of Jimmy Garner.)

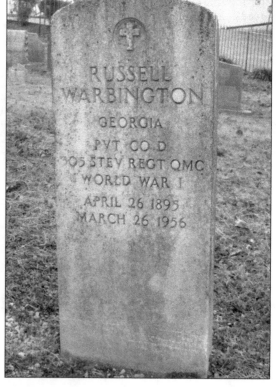

Russell Warbington (1895–1956) was a member of the Hopewell Missionary Baptist Church, and his gravestone stands in the church cemetery. He served in World War I in one of the stevedore regiments of the Quartermasters Corps. The stevedore regiments were made up of mainly African American enlisted personnel and frequently were detailed to help load and unload ships carrying munitions in ports in the United States and Europe. (Courtesy of the Authors.)

A total of five Norcross men died during service in World War II: Joseph Sharp Davidson, Aubrey Eugene Davidson, Wyly Quillian Letson, Joseph Harold Mitchell, and Ralph Westbrook. To honor their sacrifice, the community placed stone markers in Thrasher Park shortly after the war ended. These deteriorated over time, and in 2009, the city again memorialized the fallen World War II veterans, this time with bronze plaques placed in Thrasher Park. (Courtesy of Robert Byars.)

Joseph Harold Mitchell was born in 1922. Harold and his siblings were raised by their grandparents on a farm down a dirt road in the country. Today, that road is called Mitchell Road. Mitchell enlisted in the US Army in July 1942 and received the Purple Heart during his service in Sicily and North Africa. He was killed on July 11, 1944, and is buried in Normandy, France. (Courtesy of Frances Mitchell.)

Ralph Westbrook (1919–1946) was born to Berry and Apha Westbrook, one of seven children who grew up on a 300-plus-acre farm that included most of what is the current-day Peachtree Station subdivision. An enlisted man, he served on the USS *Helena*, achieving the rank of chief electrical mate. While still in service, he died from an illness contracted during the war. (Courtesy of Jane Holbrook.)

Wyly Quillian "Quill" Letson is pictured with his wife, Sarah Jeffers Letson. Quill was born in 1910 to Dr. Farmer Hinton Letson and Eva Leona Johnson Letson. He enlisted in the Navy and was killed on June 9, 1944, when the minesweeper he was aboard sank in the English Channel. (Courtesy of Richard Garner.)

Walter Raleigh Garner (1901–2001), son of James R. and Mary Lankford Garner, was an Emory Medical School graduate who began his medical practice in Gainesville around 1928 and volunteered for service in World War II at age 43. He served in the Philippines, achieving the rank of colonel. He returned to private practice after the war in Gainesville and lived to be 99 years old. (Courtesy of Richard Garner.)

The Hamilton family has lived in the Pinckneyville area of Gwinnett County for generations. Arch Hamilton (shown) served in the US Navy during World War II after graduating from Norcross High School in 1945. He was a brick mason by trade, learning the skill from his uncle Jim Adams, who was also a Norcross-area resident. Hamilton also served on the Norcross City Council. (Courtesy of Lynn Hamilton Griffeth.)

Edwin "Ed" Moulder (shown on right en route from North Africa to Sicily) was drafted by the US Army in February 1942 and served throughout World War II, until August 1945. He served in North Africa, Italy, France, and Germany. During the Battle of the Bulge, he suffered frostbite on his feet and required hospitalization for a month. Ed was raised in Norcross on North Norcross Tucker Road, but since he returned from the service in 1945, he has lived in a house on Barton Street that his family moved to in 1944. Ed is descended from German stock. Three male ancestors—Lewis, John, and Valentine Moulder—all immigrated to Britain's American colonies in the mid-1700s. They settled first in Pennsylvania before branching out to other parts of the colonies. Prior to the Civil War, another ancestor, Jacob Moulder, owned 800 acres and 10 slaves. (Courtesy of Edwin Moulder.)

Pictured is Col. Clifford Jones (1879–1974), one of three sons of Homer and Mollie Jones. He was a graduate of the West Point class of 1903. Brother Dewitt was first in his class at West Point and retired a colonel; his other brother, Tom, graduated from the US Naval Academy at Annapolis, transferred to the US Army, and achieved the rank of brigadier general. (Courtesy of Sara and Pierre Levy.)

Rufus B. Dunnigan is pictured in his Army uniform during his service in the early 1950s in Mannheim, Germany. His great-grandparents Jack and Patsy Boyce helped organize Hopewell Baptist Church. Rufus, like his father Esters Dunnigan, has been very active in Hopewell Baptist, serving as deacon, church clerk, a member of the church's finance committee, and as a Sunday school scholar. (Courtesy of Rufus Dunnigan.)

W. Harold Medlock, shown in the center with two unidentified fellow soldiers during their US Army service in Korea, was descended from pioneer Gwinnett settler Isham Medlock. During his service in Korea, Harold's assignment was to carry a 140-pound machine gun loaded with ammunition. Afterwards, he taught biology at Tucker High School and became a noted authority on the history of the Pinckneyville area. (Courtesy of Lori Medlock Anderson.)

Col. John A. Adams (1919–2009), son of the local blacksmith of the same name, served as a pilot in World War II, Korea, and the Vietnam War. He is shown holding a shotgun that is a family heirloom—it was used by his grandmother Caroline Pruitt Adams Turner (1848–1937) to kill her second husband, George Whitley. (Courtesy of Shannon Byers.)

Seven

NORCROSS GOVERNMENT

Lillian Hicks Webb was the first female member of the Norcross City Council, the first female mayor, the first female Gwinnett County commissioner, and the first woman to chair the Gwinnett County Board of Commissioners. She is shown with Bishop William Sheals of Hopewell Missionary Baptist Church and Cynthia McKinney, who was a member of the US House of Representatives representing this area for several terms. (Courtesy of Lillian Hicks Webb.)

Norcross City Hall was located on South Peachtree Street in the 1950s, as shown. The city fire truck was housed in the same building. By the 1980s, city government moved into what had previously been a post office building on Lawrenceville Street; that building was later expanded into the current city hall–police complex. (Courtesy of Jane Holbrook.)

Reuben Gant Jr. (shown) served on the Norcross City Council two different times, initially in the 1950s. After service in the US Army, he was a volunteer fireman and worked at the Carlyle Hardware Store. Gant's father, Reuben Sr., was active as a cotton broker and supplier to local farmers in Norcross in the 1920s and 1930s. (Courtesy of Reuben Gant Jr.)

Up until the 1950s, a group of local residents formed a school board for the Norcross school system, working in conjunction with the Gwinnett County Board of Education. Shown in 1957 are, from left to right, local school board members Jim Fickling, W.H. Everett, Allen Johnson, L.D. Ewing, and Earnest Humphries. Everett was also a local Boy Scout troop leader, and Johnson and Ewing served terms on the city council. Humphries, member of a longtime Norcross-area family, established the Humphries Concrete Block Company in the 1950s, helping supply the building boom that hit Gwinnett County in the later part of the 20th century. He was active in many civic organizations, including the Lions Club, Gwinnett Chamber of Commerce, and Pinckneyville Community Association. (Courtesy of Norcross High School.)

This photograph shows Georgia-born Jimmy Carter addressing a crowd at the Pinckneyville Spring Festival near Norcross in 1969. Carter went on to become governor of Georgia and then president of the United States from 1977 to 1981. The Pinckneyville Spring Festival was held in a number of locations in the Norcross area, including Jones Bridge Park after its establishment in the 1970s. (Courtesy of Lori Medlock Anderson.)

Franklin A. Dodgen (1854–1903), shown, was the popular Norcross town marshal at the turn of the 20th century. He was described as an "officer without fear" and died of a stroke at an early age. He is buried in the Norcross City Cemetery, near the downtown area. (Courtesy of Sandie Nesbit Speer.)

Joyce Blackstock Howington (1933–2007) is pictured at a 1995 Norcross Garden Club Open House with its president, Allene Richardson (right). Howington was vice president and secretary of Norcross Builders, Inc., and in 1996, she was elected to serve the first of three terms on the Norcross City Council. She was credited for applying her business and accounting acumen to the public sector. She and her husband, Carl, raised their children in Norcross, and Joyce was well known for her love of the Christmas season. The Norcross Garden Club was founded in 1958, the successor to the Norcross Civic Improvement Club, which had organized in 1916 and was dissolved in 1958. The Norcross Garden Club affiliated with the Garden Clubs of Georgia in March 1962. The first president of the Norcross Garden Club was Mrs. Kermit Maloney (Carrie), and Lillian Hicks Webb served as its first secretary. (Courtesy of the Norcross Garden Club.)

Alan "Pappy" Sudderth (1889–1949) was the town marshal of Norcross in 1916, when he encountered an unruly individual at a local carnival one night. The confrontation escalated to a shoot-out in which Sudderth was seriously injured by local farmer Jeff Staples, who died from Marshal Sudderth's return fire. (Courtesy of Richard Sudderth.)

Homer Green (1891–1938), whose gravestone in the Norcross City Cemetery is shown, was town police chief during the Prohibition era. He turned a blind eye to local bootleggers but confiscated any illicit moonshine he discovered passing through Norcross on its way from North Georgia to Atlanta. (Courtesy of the Authors.)

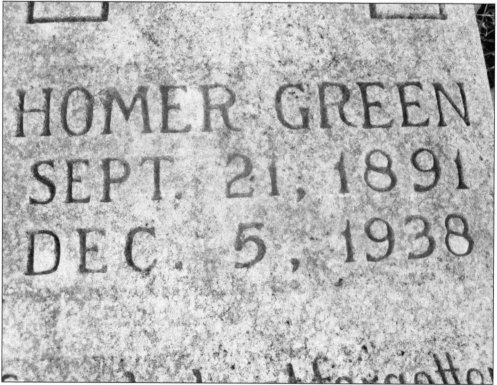

When Norcross police chief Homer Green was injured in a car accident in November 1937, the City of Norcross sent some of its council members over to Harry Simpson's farm on the Chattahoochee River in nearby Pinckneyville to call on Simpson's son Grady to fill in for the recovering chief. About a week later, Homer died, and Grady Simpson became the town's police chief. Harry Simpson purchased the Medlock House on Thrasher Street and, in 1945, deeded it to his son. Grady and his wife, Carrie Sue Westbrook Simpson, raised their family in that house, and it remained in the Simpson family until 1989. Grady Simpson is pictured; he served Norcross as its chief of police for 32 years—a position for which he had to reapply annually. Back then, most, if not all, city employees had to reapply annually for their jobs, and they did so by writing a letter to the city. Simpson also served as a volunteer firefighter for the city. (Courtesy of Jane Holbrook.)

Rossie "Tot" Brundage (1919–1982) moved to Norcross from Milledgeville, Georgia, and became a 50-year employee in the city's public works department. Brundage was the resident expert about the city's power and sewer systems. None of this information was written down; he had a magnificent memory and kept all of that information his head. After Brundage's death, the city named a park in his memory. (Courtesy of the City of Norcross.)

Local resident Gus Morton (shown) worked at the US Army's Atlanta Depot (later called Fort Gillem) during World War II, and through his connections there, he arranged for the City of Norcross to obtain a surplus Army fire truck, which the city used for many years. (Courtesy of Norcross Masonic Lodge.)

Norcross had an active volunteer fire department for many years. At first, their equipment consisted of a trailer with a hose that could be pulled to the site of a fire by a (normal) city truck. In the 1940s, the city acquired the fire truck shown behind the gathering of firefighters in this photograph from about 1955. In the early 2000s, the Norcross Car Show Committee took on the restoration of this fire truck as its number-one project. Many local men who had always tinkered on cars and trucks joined the effort to restore this truck to its original condition. This restoration process took over three years and cost more than $35,000 to complete. Once this truck was completely restored, it was given back to the city, and it is housed in the Norcross Fire Museum. (Courtesy of Gwinnett Fire Station No. 1.)

Ray Gunnin was elected to the Gwinnett County Commission in 1968. Spurred by the devastating effects of house fires in a county with a haphazard system of volunteer fire departments only covering selected areas, he pushed to establish a countywide professional fire service. The first county firefighters are shown at a station in Norcross, with chief Ray Mattison in the front left. (Courtesy of Dwayne Higgins.)

Betty Mauldin served Norcross as the city clerk from 1961 to 1994. In her early years, the clerk's office was responsible for almost all city administrative functions—planning, development and inspection, personnel, finance, billing, and collections. Mauldin is shown with her husband, Freddy, in the photograph. The city park at the corner of Lawrenceville and Jones Streets is named for her. (Courtesy of Carl Mauldin.)

Eight

EVENTS AND PERSONALITIES

This picture shows Henry M. "Doc" Lively (third from left) in front of the Keady Drug Store in downtown Norcross. Lively, a former mayor of the town, died on Christmas Day, 1915, of a shotgun blast, the resolution of an argument he had that morning with respected local butcher Bija Nuckolls. (Courtesy of Carl and Sherry Johnson.)

Originally from New York City, Frank Leavitt came to Norcross after marrying a local girl, Doris Dean. In the 1930s under the management of his wife, he achieved great success as a professional wrestler, adopting the name Man Mountain Dean—he told local resident Reuben Gant Jr. that he had made $35,000 from a single appearance during that time. He also appeared in a number of feature films. (Courtesy of Richard Garner.)

Ida Wootten (1866–1943), whose gravestone in the Norcross City Cemetery is shown, was a demanding but well-loved music teacher who organized operettas and recitals showcasing Norcross youth in Norcross in the early years of the 20th century. This monument was erected through a subscription funded by her students, this cause having been championed by Louette Johnson Rochester, a local resident. (Courtesy of the Authors.)

Brothers Frank (in the truck with a shotgun) and Harry Langford were the sons of James Lewis Langford and Alice Satterfield of Pinckneyville. Frank, whose nickname was "Shotgun," was a very colorful character and an adept storyteller. Frank and Harry owned a small cannon, and the celebratory rounds they fired every Christmas and New Year's Eve could be heard all over town. Frank and Harry were so well known as housepainters that people would wait as long as two years to have them paint their houses. It has been said that, every once in a while, the two painters would mix together whatever paint they had left over from other jobs, resulting in a rather odd color combination. In this photograph, Frank, Harry, and their dogs are preparing to go quail hunting. They took the dogs on their painting jobs as well. (Courtesy of Richard Garner.)

Oliver Oglethorpe "Ollie" Simpson Jr. was a popular figure in Norcross and around the region due to his good humor and wit. It is said that when he would go to the store or barbershop, a crowd would gather just to hear what he had to say. Here, he is speaking to a social gathering, likely the Norcross Lions Club, in the 1950s. (Courtesy of Jimmy Nesbit.)

Dr. Sylvester "Jack" Cain Jr. (1902–1965) was a beloved figure in Norcross, described in A.P. Francis's history as "genial, sympathetic, and very understanding." He attended Oglethorpe University in the 1920s, riding the Air Line Belle commuter train to class each day. He graduated from Emory Medical School in 1925 and spent the last 30 years of his life practicing medicine in Norcross. (Courtesy of the City of Norcross.)

Mrs. A.P. Francis (Blanche) was a member of the Norcross Woman's Club in the 1960s, and her husband, a non-Norcross native, undertook the task of writing a comprehensive history of the town. His interesting and detailed work drew upon a number of unidentified sources, perhaps including the Norcross Woman's Club archives, which are not generally available to historians at this time. (Courtesy of Special Collections and Archives, Georgia State University.)

Claude E. "Mutt" Ross, also known as the "Wheel Barrow Man," was a familiar figure around Norcross for much of the second half of the 20th century, walking up and down the highways of the area on a daily basis and retrieving objects of interest on the side of the road. His always-on-display medal collection included a real sheriff's badge, but most were crackerjack prizes and the like. (Courtesy of Ken Weatherford.)

The Pinckneyville Spring Festival was a popular event for a number of years in the late 1960s, 1970s, and 1980s. The festival began in 1966 and was sponsored by the Pinckneyville Community Association. This annual event was held for many years on the grounds of the historic Medlock Homestead, which used to stand near the intersection of present-day Spalding Drive and Holcomb Bridge Road at the site of the Spalding Corners shopping center. The festival was a two-day event, with arts and crafts, speakers, music, and fun for all. In keeping true to its roots, the organizers of the festival ensured that it also paid homage to Pinckneyville's important history as an early settlement in southwestern Gwinnett County. In later years, this festival was moved to Jones Bridge Park. Some proceeds of each festival helped to fund community projects. (Courtesy of Lori Medlock Anderson.)

On the evening of April 25, 1942, a passenger train with two locomotives headed north out of Atlanta but made an unplanned stop in Norcross. Local residents Irving Bailey and Butch Green were hauling a truckload of rock. Their truck got stuck at the Autry Street crossing over the Southern Railroad track and could not be removed before the collision occurred. One of the engines landed on the south side of the tracks near the Jones Street crossing, while the second was on the other side of the tracks a short distance away. The engine shown was restored and later used to pull the funeral train of Pres. Franklin Roosevelt on part of its journey in the spring of 1945. (That train came through Norcross, with Roosevelt's casket on display on the last car, so the nation's citizens could bid a final goodbye to their respected leader—an event remembered vividly to this day by many longtime Norcross residents.) This engine is now on display in the Smithsonian Institution in Washington, DC. (Courtesy of Special Collections and Archives, Georgia State University.)

In July 1996, the eyes of the world focused on Atlanta, the host of the Centennial Olympic Games. The Olympic Torch was run through several metro Atlanta neighborhoods leading up to the opening ceremony. This crowd came to Norcross to witness the torch relay pass in front of city hall, located at that time in the former post office building on Lawrenceville Street. (Courtesy of the Norcross Garden Club.)

In 1996, the Atlanta Olympic Games Torch Committee held an essay contest to award the opportunity to carry the torch as it approached the Olympic Stadium. Shelby Horn, of Norcross, was a winner in the contest, and as a result, the torch relay passed through the town. This picture shows Shelby running with the Olympic torch held high. (Courtesy of Shelby Horn.)

In the fall of 1992, Carl Johnson, a great-great-grandson of A.A. Johnson and owner of Johnson's Store on Jones Street, approached a group of men gathered by the railroad tracks in central Norcross and discovered that they were an advance team for a George H.W. Bush whistle-stop campaign swing, which was scheduled to pass through Norcross. Their plan was for the president's train to slow down, allowing him to wave to the crowd, but after Carl told them about his family and the history of Norcross, they altered the plans and arranged for the president to stop in Norcross and make a speech. Johnson's Store became "ground zero" for the event, and Secret Service men were seen throughout the city. On the day President Bush spoke, October 21, 1992, thousands came to hear him in Norcross. Bush is pictured in front of the depot. (Photograph taken by Teresa Cantrell; courtesy of Carl and Sherry Johnson.)

Newt Gingrich and John Linder, two members of the Georgia delegation to the US House of Representatives, came to Norcross as part of Pres. George H.W. Bush's campaign stop on October 21, 1992. They are pictured at the corner of South Peachtree and Jones Streets. Gingrich later served as the Speaker of the House. (Courtesy of Danny Lay.)

Shortly before midnight on April 9, 1998, a tornado ripped across metro Atlanta's Northside, reaching wind speeds of 150 miles per hour. After striking Cobb, Fulton, and DeKalb Counties, the storm touched down in Norcross, bringing heavy damage to the area. This picture shows trees downed at Norcross Presbyterian Church on Medlock Bridge Road. The length of this tornado's path was 20 miles. (Courtesy of Norcross Presbyterian Church.)

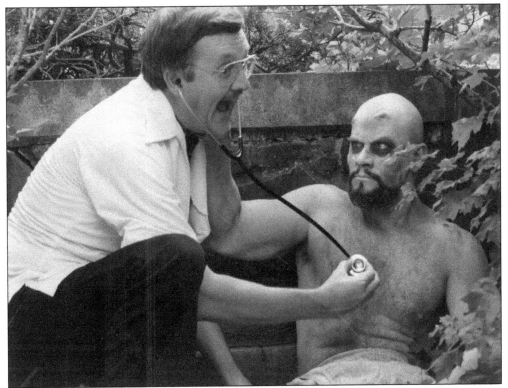

This photograph is from a cast party in a Norcross park during the filming of *Mutant* in the mid-1980s. It shows Dr. James Woods, a local veterinarian, whose offices were used as a location in the film, "examining" the actor who played the victim of pollution at a local chemical plant. (Courtesy of Dr. James Woods.)

These Gwinnett Water System towers, bearing the local marketing slogans "Gwinnett is Great" and "Success Lives Here," were a familiar sight for drivers entering Gwinnett County on Interstate 85 for 35 years. Until their removal in 2010, they stood on a hill overlooking the highway just north of Jimmy Carter Boulevard. (Courtesy of Venusnep Photography.)

Visit us at
arcadiapublishing.com